BEYOND MEDICINE

A Story of Healing, Faith and Resilience

DR. JIGNA GARASIA PATEL

INDIA · SINGAPORE · MALAYSIA

ISBN 979-8-89363-405-1

Contents

Disclaimer

This memoir chronicles my personal journey through the diagnosis, treatment, and living with a rare form of sarcoma. The experiences, decisions, and outcomes described within these pages are deeply personal and specific to my unique medical condition, circumstances, and consultations with healthcare professionals, including specialists in the United States.

It is crucial for readers to understand that the medical opinions, treatments, and decisions discussed in this book are based on my specific situation, where a defined line of treatment for my rare disease does not universally exist. The nature of rare diseases often involves navigating uncertain treatment protocols, where the course of action may vary significantly from one patient to another. In my case, a decision was made to take a break from certain treatments, a decision sanctioned by my doctor considering the intricacies of my illness and the lack of standardised treatment pathways.

This narrative should not, under any circumstances, be interpreted as medical advice or a guideline for treatment for others facing similar health issues. Every individual's health condition is unique, and treatment should always be personalised based on a thorough consultation with qualified healthcare providers. I strongly urge any patient or caregiver reading this memoir not to alter or discontinue any treatment without the explicit recommendation and supervision of their doctor or healthcare team.

In situations where treatment options seem uncertain or when considering a significant change in your treatment plan, it is imperative to seek the guidance and approval of healthcare professionals who understand your medical history and current condition. This memoir may discuss the possibility of injectable chemotherapy or other treatment modalities as part of my personal treatment plan, which was recommended based on a comprehensive evaluation of my illness by my healthcare providers.

Remember, the journey with a rare disease is fraught with challenges, including navigating through the unknown and making difficult decisions about treatment options. This memoir aims to share my story in the hope of providing support and understanding to others on similar paths. However, it is not a substitute for professional medical advice, diagnosis, or treatment.

Always seek the advice of your physician or other qualified health provider with any questions you may have regarding a medical condition. Never disregard professional medical advice or delay in seeking it because of something you have read in this book.

Foreword

Life has a way of surprising us, taking us on journeys we never expected to go on. Dr Jigna Garasia Patel's memoir is one such journey, telling the story of her fight against a rare disease. It's not just about the medical battles she faced, but about her incredible strength, hope, and the power of never giving up.

I've had the pleasure of working with Dr. Nitin Patel at Vaidik Dental College, Daman, for over fourteen years, and it's through him that I've seen Dr. Jigna's journey up close. Meeting her at the annual function of our college was just the beginning. Little did I know her story would leave such a lasting impression on me.

Dr. Jigna's story is an important one for many reasons. It shows us that healing is about more than just medicine. It's about the strength of our spirit, the support of those around us, and sometimes, exploring paths beyond traditional medicine.

Through my years in healthcare, as a Padma Shri awardee, and in various leadership roles, I've seen many stories of healing. But Dr. Jigna's story stands out because it reminds us of the human side of medicine. It's about facing challenges with courage and always holding on to hope.

This memoir is a message to anyone facing tough times. It tells us that even when things seem dark, there is a way forward. Dr. Jigna didn't just face her illness head-on; she explored every avenue to find healing, showing us the power of resilience.

In reading her story, you'll find not just a journey through illness but a guide to finding light in the darkest of times. It's a reminder that, no matter what we face, we have the strength within us to overcome it.

I hope that as you read this memoir, you'll find inspiration, courage, and the reminder that life, with all its ups and downs, is worth fighting for.

With respect and admiration,
Padmashree
Dr. S.S. Vaishya
MBBS MD
Vaidik Dental College
Daman

Writing a foreword for Jigna's memoir feels like retracing the steps of a journey that has been both challenging and incredibly enriching. Our story, like many, began in a rather traditional manner—through an arranged marriage. If someone had told me then that our journey together would unfold in the way it has, I might not have believed them. We were, after all, as different as could be—her vibrant, extroverted nature contrasting sharply with my more reserved and introspective disposition. Yet, it's these differences that have become our greatest strength, binding us together in ways I could have never imagined.

Over the last 22 years, Jigna and I have navigated life's unpredictable waters together, facing highs and lows that have tested our resolve, our patience, and our love for each other. Through it all, Jigna's battle with a rare disease stands out as a period that not only tested our limits but also brought out the depth of our commitment to one another.

As a pathologist and someone deeply entrenched in the medical field, my approach to Jigna's diagnosis was, initially, clinical. I believed in the power of medicine to heal, to solve problems, and to offer solutions. Yet, as we delved deeper into the complexities of her condition, I realised that healing was about much more than just treating symptoms. It was about hope, resilience, and the strength we drew from each other.

Jigna's memoir is not just a recounting of her battle with illness; it is a testament to her indomitable spirit, her unwavering courage, and her boundless capacity for hope. It is also a story of our journey together, of the challenges we faced, and of the countless ways in which Jigna's strength inspired me.

In her darkest moments, Jigna found light not only within herself but in the world around her. She embraced alternative healing practices with an open heart and mind, seeking solace in meditation, mantras, and the wisdom of different cultures and traditions. Through her journey, I learned the true meaning of support and care—realising that sometimes, being there for someone means standing by their side, even when the path ahead is uncertain.

Jigna's memoir is a powerful reminder that life, with all its unpredictability, is a journey worth taking. Her story is one of love, hope, and the incredible strength of the human spirit. As her husband, I have had the privilege of witnessing her transformation, of seeing her face each challenge with grace and emerge stronger each time.

I trust that while perusing this memoir, you will draw inspiration from Jigna's resilience, courage, and steadfast optimism. Her narrative shines as a source of hope, reminding us that even in the face of the greatest challenges, the human spirit is capable of remarkable strength.

With all my love and admiration,
Dr. Nitin Patel
MBBS MD Pathology
Neelkanth Clinical Laboratory
Killa Pardi-396125
Gujarat

This memoir by Dr. Jigna is a personal story of a successful 'doctor's battle against a fatal disease. The grit and determination she has shown are sources of inspiration and motivation for all.

Makes for interesting reading.

Dr. Kishore Nadkarni
MBBS MS
Andrologist, Sexual Medicine Expert
Nadkarni Hospital & Test Tube Baby Centre
Killa Pardi Gujarat

My mom has always been an inspiration to me, but nothing could have prepared me for the strength she showed when she was diagnosed with a desmoid tumor. It was a terrifying time, but through it all, she never lost hope. Her resilience and bravery are described in her new book, a testament to the human spirit's ability to overcome immense challenges. It's not just a story about illness; it's a story about facing life's hardships face-to-face and emerging stronger on the other side. You should read her book to be reminded that even in the darkest moments, there is always light at the end of the tunnel. And who knows her story might just inspire you to write your own.

Naisargi Patel
Welham Girls School
Dehradun

Preface

Why did I decide to write this book? When I was facing my own tough times, finding a success story felt like finding a lifeline. So, this book is my way of throwing that lifeline to others. It's here to say, You're not alone, and Don't give up. I didn't write it for fame. It's all about offering support and inspiration.

This book isn't just my story. It's about discovering the real me along the way. Before my illness, I didn't really know my own strength. But facing this rare sarcoma taught me who I am: someone who doesn't back down, no matter how hard things get.

So, what's inside these pages? It's a simple message: we all have the strength inside us to face big challenges. My journey shows that even when things look bad, there's always a way through.

This book is for anyone fighting their own battles. It's a reminder that giving up is not in our nature. We keep trying, no matter what.

I hope my story helps you see the strength you have inside. Remember, no one has to face tough times alone. Together, we can make it through anything.

I'm deeply grateful to my dear friends Dr. Aditi Nadkarni, Dr. Foram Patel, Dr. Saurabh Gandhi, Dr. Bibek, Dr. Himanshu Chaudhary, Dr. Kirti Garg, Dr. Deepika Ghai, and my best friends Bhagvati, Pinki, Hasu, and Rupinder for all your support during this journey and for helping me write this book.

Warmly,
Dr. Jigna Garasia Patel
MBBS MD
FICOG, Reproductive Medicine
Gynaecologist & Obstetrician
Infertility Specialist
Nadkarni Hospital & Test Tube Baby Centre
Killa Pardi 396125 Gujarat

Chapter 1

Life Is a Box Full of Surprises

In the quiet of our terrace garden, with just the soft hum of the evening and the glow from the lights around us, I, Jigna, took a moment to soak in the peace with my husband, Nitin, and our daughter, Naisargi. We had just wrapped up a busy day with two big celebrations: our housewarming and Naisargi's birthday. It felt good to sit back and take it all in.

Nitin broke the silence first. "Thank God we managed to get the housewarming and Naisargi's birthday done together," he said, sounding relieved. It was great seeing everyone having a good time.

I nodded, agreeing with him." Yes, and everyone seemed to enjoy it. That's what matters."

Our daughter, all excited, joined in. "I love my new room! It's all Barbie-themed. It's like a dream come true!"

Laughing, I responded, "You are our Barbie, betu."

Nitin smiled at her. "You're the most precious doll in our life."

Just then, a sharp pain hit me out of nowhere. "Ouch, I'm in pain," I complained. "It hurts a lot."

Nitin immediately got worried. "Let's see what we can do about it. You shouldn't be in pain."

Right there, in the middle of a beautiful evening, that sudden pain was a stark reminder of life's unpredictable nature. And as I sat there, trying to smile through the discomfort, my thoughts drifted to the beginning of my story. It started in a small village in South Gujarat, close to Surat, back in 1977. Being the eldest daughter in a humble family, my life was always a mix of simple joys and big dreams.

Growing up, my father's unfulfilled aspirations hung like a quiet shadow over our household. He had dreamed of becoming a doctor, but financial limitations had steered his life down a different path. His tales of ambition and resilience shaped my childhood, igniting a fire in me that grew stronger each year.

As a young girl, my days were filled with the usual routine of school and play, but there was always an underlying current of something more, a sense of destiny that seemed to be guiding me. This feeling crystallised when I entered B.J. Medical College in Ahmedabad, choosing to specialise in gynaecology. It was more than a career choice; it was an acclamation to my father's unfinished dream and a commitment to a cause greater than myself.

By 2004, I was deeply entrenched in my role as an IVF consultant. My life was a reflection of my personality – dedicated, focused, and somewhat introverted. Work was my passion, and there was little room for anything else. But life had a way of balancing itself out.

In 2002, I found my life partner in Dr. Nitin Patel, a pathologist who not only shared my professional values but also brought a sense of balance and joy to my personal life. Our journey to parenthood was not straightforward, marred by challenges and setbacks. However, in 2008, our perseverance was rewarded with the birth of our daughter, Naisargi. She was more than just a child to us; she was a symbol of hope, a testament to our struggles and ultimate triumph.

My family, though compact, was a stronghold of support and love. Professionally, I was fortunate enough to have mentors like Dr. Purnima Nadkarni and Dr. Kishore Nadkarni, who were instrumental in shaping my career.

The year 2016 brought with it a significant milestone. I achieved a long-held dream of owning a bungalow. To celebrate, we planned a grand event on January 27th, combining our housewarming with my daughter Naisargi's birthday. It was intended to be a joyous occasion, a celebration of new beginnings, but as life would have it, it was also the eve of a new, unforeseen challenge.

Our new home, adorned in white as I had always envisioned, stood as an affirmation of our efforts and dreams. The only exception was my daughter's room, vibrant and colourful, reflecting her youthful spirit. My aspiration for a soothing, calm sanctuary had been fulfilled. Adding to this, I realised another dream—not one, but two terrace gardens. The day began with a small pooja in the morning, and by evening, the house was bustling with guests for my daughter's birthday celebration.

That day, our house was filled with laughter, friends, and family, all enjoying the party. Everyone said it was a beautiful home, and I felt so proud. But I didn't know that this happiness was about to be challenged. After the event, I started feeling a sharp pain in my belly. At first, I thought it was just a urine infection. That happens sometimes, right? So, I started taking the usual medicines. But the pain didn't go away. It was strange and worrying. After examining my symptoms, Dr. Akshay Nadkarni suspected that it could be appendicitis and recommended further investigation. I was admitted to the hospital, where a series of tests were conducted. Despite all efforts, the reports came back frustratingly normal, leaving me confused about the cause of my ongoing discomfort.

Then Dr. Akshay suggested doing a laparoscopy. It's a small operation with a camera to see what's happening inside. I was a bit scared, thinking it might be something serious. The doctors went in, thinking they might need to fix my appendix. But what they found was something else. To everyone's surprise, including mine, he discovered and biopsied a small mass. This unexpected finding turned out to be a life-saving decision, as it led to early detection and timely treatment. I will forever be grateful for Dr. Akshay's expertise and intuition, which played a significant role in preserving my health and well-being.

The report was something none of us were prepared for—a Desmoid tumour. A rare disease, one among 7,000, often misdiagnosed or undiagnosed due to its rarity and lack of awareness even within the medical community. As a gynaecologist married to a pathologist, we were both unaware of it.

The atmosphere changed palpably. I could sense the tension, and see the strained smiles of those around me as they grappled with the news. Dr. Aditi Nadkarni's suggestion of antitubercular drugs and Dr. Shashi Heranjal's revelation about the mass felt surreal. Only days ago, we were celebrating my daughter's 8th birthday and our new home, and now, we were facing an uncertain journey.

Desmoid tumours, like 90% of rare diseases, lack a cure or FDA-approved treatment. The treatment journey is often a trial-and-error process involving multiple therapies. What works for one patient may not work for another, adding to the complexity and emotional toll of the disease.

Desmoid tumours are tricky. There's no one way to treat them. What works for one person might not work for another. And this tumour was a sly one. It grows slowly and doesn't spread like other cancers, but it can still be very harmful because of the areas around which it grows.

So, there I was, fresh from one of the happiest moments in my new house, stepping into a journey full of uncertainties. My family and I were just beginning to understand what this diagnosis meant. It was a big change, and we were getting ready to face whatever was coming our way.

My symptoms, you see, had only been around for a week or so. But being a doctor myself, I could tell something wasn't right. The blood tests and sonography all came back normal, which should've been good news. But deep down, I just knew something was off. It's funny how sometimes you just know these things. That gut feeling, along with Dr. Akshay Nadkarni's careful approach during the laparoscopy, led us to find the tumour.

I often think about that day. If Dr. Akshay hadn't been so thorough, if he hadn't decided to check beyond what seemed like a normal appendix, things could have been much worse. The tumour, it turned out, was entangled with a blood vessel near my bowels. That's what was causing all the pain.

After finding out about the tumour, my head was spinning. One minute we were celebrating Naisargi's birthday and our new home, and the next, I was dealing with this tornado. It felt so sudden and unreal. I reached out to some old colleagues and mentors from my residency days at Gujarat Cancer and Research Institute in Ahmedabad. But my condition was so rare that they didn't have many answers either.

The uncertainty of it all was really tough. I kept thinking about my work. Being an IVF consultant and obstetrician isn't easy. It's a busy, demanding job. I was always on call, always ready to help my patients. The thought of not being able to do that, or maybe having to slow down, was scary. I started thinking about maybe just doing consultations, but even that felt overwhelming, considering what I was going through. The questions about my future just wouldn't leave me alone. Will I be able to live a normal life again? What's going to happen to me? These thoughts kept swirling in my mind, day and night. The more I spoke to doctors, the more anxious I would get. Most of them told me they hadn't seen a case like mine in their entire careers. That kind of news doesn't exactly put your mind at ease, you know?

I was desperate for someone, anyone, to tell me they'd seen this before and knew what to do. But no one could give me that assurance. It was like walking in the dark, not knowing where the path led to.

The uncertainty was the hardest part. Every time I talked to a doctor about treatment options or what to expect, I was left with more questions than answers. And there was this big question helicoptering over me all the time—about life and death. It wasn't just about whether I would survive, but about how my life would be from now on.

When I first found out about my illness, advice came from all sides. After spending hours on Google, one thing became crystal clear: this wasn't just about whether the disease was cancerous or not. The real deal was finding doctors who specialise in the treatment, no matter what. I also learned that when it comes to cancer medicine, it's pretty much trying things out to see what works.

The biggest shocker was finding out that my type of disease could come back 80-90% of the time within five years. That hit me hard. It made me think what my game plan here was? Because really, who knows what five years down the line looks like? This thought kept me up at night, worrying about money, health, and what was going on in my head.

All this time, I kept looking up stuff about my condition online, trying to find anything that could help. But most times, all I got were more questions and a whole lot of worry. I've always been someone who loves doing a million things at once, staying busy, and being out there helping people. So, the thought of not being able to do my job as a gynaecologist because of my health scared me more than anything. My job's not the kind where you can just take it easy. If I'm not well, I can't be there for my patients.

But here's the thing—during this tough period, my patients were amazing. They kept coming to me, not just for gynaecology stuff but for advice on other health issues too. Knowing they trusted me that much, even when I was fighting my own battle, meant everything. It showed me I could still make a difference, and still be the doctor they wanted, even with everything going on.

So, what I learned from digging into my diagnosis and trying to figure out the next steps was huge. That's when I found the Desmoidian group on Facebook. It was a game-changer. The group was full of people who had been through what I was going through. They discussed their treatments, how they managed day-to-day life, and how their caregivers supported them. It was like finding a treasure trove of information and support.

From them, I learned that in many parts of the world, desmoid tumours are treated by sarcoma specialists. But here in India, at that time, that kind of expertise was hard to find. It was a whole new angle to consider and something I hadn't heard from any of the doctors I'd spoken to.

Connecting with the Desmoidian community gave me a sense of not being alone in this. It also opened my eyes to different treatment approaches and the importance of being proactive about my health. It was a tough time, filled with uncertainties and fear, but finding this community was like finding a ray of hope in a very stormy sea.

This journey with the Desmoidian group on Facebook was an eye-opener. I realised that even though my tumour wasn't spreading like typical cancers, it was just as serious. It was a big moment for me—understanding that I needed to see an oncologist, go through all those big tests like CT scans and MRIs, and maybe deal with the same side effects that cancer patients face. It was scary to think about, but I knew it was what I had to do.

So, I made up my mind to treat this tumour like a malignant tumour. This decision, this change in how I saw my condition, turned out to be really important. After 11 months, the tumour came back, and this time it was more aggressive. I stuck to my doctor's advice, even though the side effects were tough, it was crucial to keep the disease under control.

Looking back, I see how important it was to choose laparoscopy for that first check. It might have seemed simpler to go for an open surgery, but the laparoscopy gave the doctors a better look at everything inside, making sure they didn't miss anything.

Now, when I talk to other people with Desmoid Tumours, I always tell them to take it seriously right from the start. A lot of them were told at first that their tumours were benign, which meant they waited longer to get the right kind of treatment. But with Desmoid Tumours, waiting can make things a lot tougher. Once the symptoms get bad and the tumour gets bigger, treating it can be really tough.

You know, despite everything, I never gave up. Sure, each day came with its own hurdles, but there were also those little wins, those glimpses of hope that kept me going. My family was incredible through it all—always by my side, always cheering me on. Their love and support, along with the encouragement from the Desmoidian community, really kept me moving forward.

Sometimes, I'd sit in our terrace garden in the evening, watching the sun go down. The sky would turn this beautiful golden colour, so peaceful and calm. It was such a contrast to the storm I was living through. But in those quiet moments, I found peace. It was a peace that came from accepting what was happening and being determined to face whatever was coming next.

Chapter 2

Facing the Unknown

So, there we were, my husband and I, holding a report that spelt out a rare condition, something not commonly seen in our part of the world. With just 2-4 cases per million each year and more common in the West, it felt like we had drawn an unusual hand in life's unpredictable game. We decided to head to Ahmedabad, the place where I spent my medical school days, to consult with a top cancer surgeon. Surgery was on the cards, and we wanted the best hands for the job.

Ahmedabad had a certain familiarity, but the situation we were walking into was anything but less than a war. The onco surgeon, Dr. J. J. Patel we met, was straightforward in his communication. He compared the tumour to an unwanted guest at a party, freely mingling with any organ it pleased. And my vague back pain? That could be the tumour getting a bit too cosy with crucial nerves. We couldn't take any chances. If the situation became too complicated and the surgery went off course, I might face the risk of paralysis or other serious complications. So, we dived headfirst into a whirlpool of tests—CT scans, MRI of the spine—leaving no stone unturned.

I knew this was going to involve my bowels, and the thought was unsettling. You see, the bowel is like the unsung hero of the body—mess with it, and you're looking at a lifetime of issues.

My hope was straightforward yet profound: remove the tumour while preserving the integrity of the bowels.

In March 2016, I faced the most gruelling challenge of my life—a surgery that was nothing short of a marathon. For an excruciating 6-7 hours, surgeons worked to remove a significant portion of my intestines, 45 centimetres, to be precise. But the surgery was just the beginning of a tumultuous journey I never asked for.

But this story isn't just about the physical ordeal. It's about the emotional marathon my loved ones ran alongside me. My friend Dr Pinki and her husband Dr Nimesh, Dr Akshay Nadkarni, my anaesthetist Dr Shashi Heranjal, my sister Vaishali, Dipak—my sister Vibhuti's husband, all there, anchored by hope and shared tension, as Nitin and my dad awaited the outcome. Imagine their psychological turmoil, especially when the surgeons, at one point, deemed the situation inoperable. There I was, under anaesthesia, oblivious to the world, sleeping through a storm while my dear ones weathered it with bated breath in the waiting area.

In a gesture that truly shows friendship, Dr. Himanshu Rana, my physician friend, made it a point to be by my side in the ICU. After a long day's work at his own hospital, he came to monitor my condition through the night, ensuring I received the best care possible. It's during moments like these that you realise the immense blessings of having such a supportive circle of friends and family. Each one of them, in their own way, contributed to my recovery, fuelling my fight with love, care, and unwavering support. Their collective efforts, their emotional investment, and their presence were my pharos of hope in one of the darkest times of my life.

I came home from the hospital on the eighth day after my surgery. The days right after the operation went by without any problems. We had gotten the green light for my health insurance before the surgery. But on the day I was supposed to leave the hospital, they suddenly said that because it was cancer, I couldn't use my insurance. I couldn't believe it; it was already 4 pm, and I just wanted to be home, especially since the next day was Holi. I had been looking forward to being with my daughter, who had been staying with her grandparents for the past 9 days. It was the first time she had been away from me like this. Somehow, we managed to sort everything out and I was discharged. Holi is my daughter's most loved festival, and we decided to celebrate it as if nothing was wrong, filling it with colours and joy just like we always do.

What followed was a rollercoaster I hadn't signed up for. Within the span of 10 days post-surgery, I was 10 kg lighter, a testimony to the struggle my body was enduring to mend itself. Those days were like a blur of pain and sleepless nights. My dad, my angel, would sit by my side, reading the Bhagavad Gita. Some nights, his voice was the only thing that could lull me to sleep. About a month later, I ventured back to the hospital, to see patients who had been waiting for me. That night, after what felt like an eternity, I slept like a baby. Despite being weak, and unable to even write properly, the happiness I saw in my patients' eyes gave me a strength I never knew I had. It pushed me to keep going to the hospital, even if just for a few hours a day. And you know what? It helped. I started getting better, faster.

I have to say, I wouldn't have made it through without Dr Purnima Nadkarni and Dr Aditi Nadkarni. They were my guardians, stepping in to handle my emergencies and surgeries, and taking care of my patients. They were more than colleagues – they were like family.

The road to recovery was long and winding. My stitches, oh boy, they were a saga. Dr. Akshay had to redo them twice. Eventually, I just asked him to let nature take its course. It worked – two months later, I was finally stitched up properly.

Keeping myself busy became my mantra during this time. It gave me purpose and kept my mind off the pain. My daughter, just nine at the time, became my little warrior. I even took her to a temple one day and laid it all out for her – my illness, the whole nine yards. It was time for her to learn some independence, just in case.

With all the support, my mind cleared enough to better understand my situation post-surgery. I talked to many doctors, but my unusual health problems often confused them. I knew there was a big chance the problem could come back, and I prepared myself, thinking I might have five years before it could happen again.

I started facing a challenge with controlling my bowel movements. If I felt the urge, I had to rush to the bathroom immediately to avoid an embarrassing situation. This problem made it hard for me to go back to my usual activities. To handle this, I created a simple plan. Whenever I was out doing errands, I wouldn't eat anything. This way, I could avoid sudden trips to the bathroom. Then, in the evening, when I was back at home or in a hotel where I felt comfortable, I would eat my meals. This routine allowed me to manage my condition better, and I still follow it today.

I also made some big changes to my diet. I stopped eating wheat, flour, bread, and almost all types of food from outside.

Around this time, we had planned an international trip with our parents, which we had booked in December 2015 to save money.

As the trip got closer, my family started to worry about how my health issues might affect the trip. They thought it might be best to cancel.

But I didn't want to cancel the trip. Despite not knowing what was wrong with me or what my future looked like, I wanted to go. I saw the trip as more than just a vacation. It was my way of showing that despite the challenges, life doesn't stop. I wanted to make lasting memories with my family. So, we went on the trip to Singapore, just going with the flow and seeing where it took us.

Fuelled by the success and joy of our Singapore journey, I harboured another wish, one that spoke to my core as a nature lover—to visit Kenya. The wild, untamed beauty of Kenya's landscapes and wildlife had always called to me, placing it at the top of my bucket list. I half-jokingly warned my husband, Nitin, that if I passed without seeing Kenya, my soul would never let him be at peace.

Thus, with a mix of determination and a touch of madness, we planned our Kenyan safari for Diwali in October 2016.

As a doctor, I am fully aware of the risks associated with travelling so soon after major surgery. Just six months post-operation, with a 20 cm vertical scar still healing, the idea of starting such an adventure might appear reckless to many. The risk of developing an incisional hernia was real, yet my desire to experience the wonders of Kenya outweighed the fears. My decision was driven not by a disregard for medical advice but by a deep-seated need to embrace life fully, to experience joy and wonder in the face of adversity.

Kenya did not disappoint. The experience was transformative, a true healing journey amidst nature's marvels. Witnessing lions, elephants, zebras, flamingoes, and wild buffalos in their natural habitat was a reminder of the beauty and resilience of life in nature. Watching wild animals in their natural habitat, I found an unexpected teacher: uncertainty. It's a wild, unpredictable dance—much like the animals I observed, each moment for them is lived fully, without worry for the next. This raw, untamed lesson made me rethink everything.

You see, these creatures, they don't stress about what's coming. They're all in, every second because in the wild, there is no guarantee of a 'next moment.' Watching them, I couldn't help but draw parallels to my own life. Here I was, tangled in worries about the future, about things entirely out of my control, while these animals simply.. lived. It hit me then, like a scene straight out of a movie, echoing Shah Rukh Khan's famous line from Kal

Ho Naa Ho – live as if there's no tomorrow. It's a line we've all heard, maybe even smiled at, but out there, in the silence of the wild, it sank in deeper. Why worry about a moment that hasn't arrived? Why not embrace the now with everything we've got?

These trips, to Singapore and Kenya, were more than just escapes from the realities of my illness. They were affirmations of life, of the beauty that exists in the world, and of the precious moments we share with those we love. They taught me that healing can come in many forms, sometimes from the most unexpected sources. Through the laughter, the adventures, and even the challenges, I found a deeper appreciation for the gift of each new day.

As I look back on those journeys, I realise they were integral to my healing process, not just physically but emotionally and spiritually. They reminded me that, amidst the trials and uncertainties, there is always room for joy, for wonder, and for love. They were journeys of the heart, each step a testament to the enduring power of hope and the unbreakable spirit of the human soul.

After the surgery in 2016, I thought the hardest part was over. But life had other plans. Just when I started to get back on my feet, a new set of challenges appeared. Two months post-surgery, I was diagnosed with gallstones. It felt like just as one problem was ending, another was beginning. And then, within a month, kidney stones appeared, along with kidney function issues. The stone got obstructed, and my kidney health took a hit. It felt like my body was a battleground, and I was caught in the crossfire. Amidst all this, my bowel got obstructed. I couldn't eat anything without pain and vomiting, and I lost a significant amount of weight again.

I also reached out to Tata Hospital (surgical department) in the mix, hoping they could shed some light. Maybe offer insights on my condition or share survivor tales. But instead, the consultant suggested a few more tests.

Going to that hospital is like running through a maze, especially when you're trying to get to your consultant. First, you've got to set up a file, then get a payment card, load it with cash, and finally, a doctor-in-training comes over to take down your whole medical history. When it was my turn, as I started answering her questions, I couldn't help it – tears just started rolling down my cheeks. The doctor-in-training looked surprised and asked me, "How can you cry being a doctor?" That moment hit me hard. Just because I'm a doctor, does that mean I don't get to feel scared or hopeless? Her question made me snap back to reality, and I quickly wiped away my tears, trying to seal back that vulnerability. It was as if she expected me to be immune to the fear and uncertainty that comes with being on this side of the diagnosis. It's one thing to be a patient, but answering those questions about my own health, knowing the full weight of each answer, was overwhelming.

I went through all the hoops without making a fuss, and finally, I was in the consultant's room. He suggested even more tests. Being a pathologist's wife, I thought it made sense to ask if we could do them back home instead. Maybe it was how I asked, or maybe he was just having a bad day, but he didn't take my question well. He practically threw my file on the table, cutting our conversation short.

Walking out of there, I felt heavier than when I'd entered. It was as if every bit of hope got sucked out of the room the moment he dismissed my file. The questions without answers, the endless tests, and now this—a consultant who wouldn't even entertain a simple request. It all piled up, leaving me drowning in negativity and despair. It felt like I was losing grip on life, with every door slamming shut in my face, and no one willing to listen or help me find a way forward.

In the span of 11 months, I underwent three CT scans. And then, the news I dreaded the most arrived – the tumour was back. We rushed to my onco surgeon Dr. J. J. Patel in Ahmedabad. He suggested surgery, which seemed to be the only option at that time. But when I heard 'surgery' again, my heart sank. I wasn't prepared for this. I needed time to think.

Heading back home, feeling so down, it was like the ground beneath me was falling apart, bit by bit. Before the report, I had convinced myself that I had five years to live life to the fullest. But now, doctors are labelling my slow-growing tumour as 'aggressive'. I felt helpless and worried. My husband and I were running around, trying to find a solution, while our daughter Naisargi, just nine years old, stayed with her grandparents and caretaker.

Despite everything, I tried to remain strong. But the suffering seemed endless. Sometimes, I found myself crying in the hospital, haunted by the uncertainty of life. Thoughts about my daughter's future without me were the hardest. She was approaching her teenage years – a time when she would need her mother the most. How could I be there for her?

I sought opinions from every corner of the country. The unanimous answer was surgery, but I wasn't ready for it. I remembered my postoperative periods – the fear, the pain. I even visited almost all the biggest hospitals in India, hoping for a different solution, but the answer was the same. The doctors warned me of dire consequences without surgery, but I refused. Having seen patients suffer post-surgery during my postgraduation at the Gujarat Cancer Research Institute, I knew the complications all too well. One major complication I feared was a colostomy, where you pass stool through an opening on your abdominal wall. Living with a stoma bag and relying on a caregiver for personal care was something I wanted to avoid at all costs. I had seen the suffering it caused firsthand.

So, with a heavy heart, I decided against the third surgery. It was a tough decision, but I felt it was the right one for me. I came home, feeling like I was losing the battle.

As I sensed my life slipping away, I began exploring alternative therapies. It was a step into the unknown, but I was ready to try anything that might offer relief and hope. It was a journey of self-discovery, looking beyond conventional medicine, and finding new ways to fight this relentless battle.

During this entire ordeal, my family was my backbone. They were always there, bringing me different therapies, trying to find something, anything, that would help. I could feel their love and concern. But, one day, I just had enough. I was taking 30 tablets a day, each with its own set of side effects. It was overwhelming. I remember snapping one day, declaring that I wasn't going to take any more medication. It was just too much.

Complications continued. I had severe diarrhoea and vomiting episodes, a routine struggle post-surgery. Sometimes I managed with oral medicines, sometimes hospitalisation was needed.

I remember one particular day, after a day at the OPD, I came home and suffered severe diarrhoea followed by weakness. It was just my daughter and me at home. I received a call about a patient who was bleeding after a normal delivery. The most critical situation in any delivery. Despite feeling weak and dizzy, I decided to go to the hospital with my daughter. As no other doctor was available due to some reason. After attending to the patient and saving her life, I collapsed from exhaustion and fluid loss. I was wheeled into the ICU, while my staff, my daughter, and the patient's relatives were in tears. To this day, I wonder if what I did was right, but at that moment, no other doctor was available.

Chapter 3

Seeking New Horizons

Nothing is permanent, not even our problems. I kept going, through the darkest nights, holding onto the hope of seeing the sunrise someday. As my journey with the disease continued, my family became more involved in exploring various treatment options. It was a time of collective brainstorming and research, everyone eager to find something that would make a difference. What to do and how to proceed were the constant questions we struggled with.

Around this time, an unexpected ray of hope appeared. Dr. Vishal Pandya, a dentist from Killa Pardi, living in the USA, an old friend from my B.J. Medical College days in Ahmedabad, and his wife Priyanka learned about my condition. Priyanka, in her determination to help, set out on a mission to find the best doctor for my specific tumour. Her efforts led her to an Indian-origin sarcoma consultant based in the USA. I can never forget the day she gave me his mobile number—it felt like I was standing at a crossroads, with a new path unfolding before me.

I remember holding the phone, my heart pounding with a mix of hope and anxiety. In the USA, direct access to doctors isn't as straightforward as in India. Would he answer my call? If he did, would he be willing to listen to my story? Would he offer any advice over the phone? With these thoughts racing through my mind, I dialled the number.

To my surprise, he answered on the first ring. The background noise hinted he was somewhere lively, perhaps at a party, yet his voice was calm and focused. I could almost picture him stepping away from the crowd, finding a quiet corner just for our conversation. As I poured out my worries, I felt a wave of relief wash over me, like a comforting embrace from an old friend. He listened with the kind of attention that made the miles between us disappear. Then, he dropped the bombshell that would pivot the direction of my treatment.

In the USA, he explained, they approach this type of tumour differently. No scalpels, no operating rooms. Instead, he suggested a groundbreaking medication called Imatinib, a name that was unfamiliar to me but quickly became my source of hope. Commonly used for blood and kidney cancers, this little pill could be the key to turning my story around. His words weren't just advice; they were a lifeline, pulling me towards a future I hadn't dared to imagine. So, with excitement and a bit of trepidation, I embarked on this new journey towards healing. After I hung up the phone, I stood there in the quiet, feeling his words sink in deep. This was a big moment. I was filled with all sorts of feelings: hope, worry, and even a little thrill about what could happen next.

Taking this new medicine, Imatinib, wasn't just about trying something new. It was about stepping into the unknown, hoping for a change. The thought of a medicine I'd never heard of before helping me out seemed almost too good to be true. How could one little pill offer so much hope?

Armed with the promise of a new beginning, my husband and I wasted no time. We knew we needed to act quickly to get our hands on Imatinib, the medicine that suddenly felt like a key to a locked door. So, we started reaching out to cancer specialists, explaining my situation and the conversation I had with the doctor from the USA. We were determined to find someone who could prescribe this medication, someone who understands our urgency and hope. However, we were met with resistance. Due to the rarity of the tumour and a lack of experience with it, most doctors were hesitant. They insisted that surgery was the only option, mentioning that the tumour is chemoresistant and radioresistant. I felt like I was hitting a wall at every turn. With only about 250 registered patients like me in the country, many doctors were hearing about this condition for the first time.

After much thought and discussion with my local physician, I decided to start Imatinib on my own. It was a bold move, but I felt it was necessary. I requested my physician to provide primary treatment for any side effects or complications, taking full responsibility for any outcomes.

But to proceed with this new course of treatment, I needed it in writing, and for that, I applied for a US visa. It was a step filled with uncertainty, but it was a step I needed to take. After a whirlwind of discussions, advice from friends, and consultations with doctors, I stumbled upon MD Anderson Hospital. Known for its cutting-edge treatments and research, it felt like a light of hope in a sea of uncertainty. Taking a deep breath, I reached out to their international centre, hopeful yet apprehensive about what they might say. The response was a mix of hope and a daunting reality: a treatment plan estimated at around 35,00,000 rupees, not including the costs for flights, accommodation, and everything else. They suggested a month-long stay.

Sitting down to look at my finances, I realised I had about 30,00,000 rupees in savings. The decision to proceed wasn't easy.

The possibilities of what could have been swirled in my mind like a relentless storm. What if the treatment didn't work? What if my tumour remained unresponsive? I knew what I was battling by then, and the thought of spending all my savings on a chance—on a possibility—was terrifying. But on the flip side, what if it worked? I could earn back the money spent, but only if the treatment gave me that chance.

Amidst these thoughts, life at home was a whirlwind of wedding preparations. My cousin Sweety was getting married, and the air was filled with excitement and joy. Yet, amidst the celebration, my husband, parents, and I were caught in a whirlpool of confusion and fear, our hearts heavy with uncertainty.

Noticing our distress, my uncle and aunt—Nayna Foi and Navneet Fua—pulled us aside, their eyes filled with concern. I poured out my fears and the monumental decision we faced. Without hesitation, my uncle, with a generosity that left me speechless, offered to cut down on the wedding expenses and give us the money needed for the treatment. His words were a lifeline, a moment of incredible kindness that cut through the fog of my fears.

I was left speechless, overwhelmed by this gesture of selfless support. It was more than just financial help; it was a testament to the strength of family bonds, to the love that holds us up in our darkest times. This moment, this decision to reach out to MD Anderson, became not just my leap of faith but ours as a family. It was a step into the unknown, fuelled by the hope of what could be, and bolstered by the unconditional support of loved ones.

Embarking on this journey to MD Anderson, we were filled with a mixture of fear and hope. The uncertainties were many, but the possibility of finding a treatment that could change the course of my illness made every risk worth taking. It was a collective decision, a shared journey, underscored by the belief that when we come together, even the most daunting challenges can be faced.

Chapter 4

The Unsaid

In this long journey with my illness, I've always felt that my family, especially my husband, bore the brunt of the struggle. While I battled the disease physically, they fought on every other front. My husband, a man of few words, found himself in a storm of responsibilities. He was the rock, ensuring we had the financial means for my treatments and securing our daughter's future. All the while, he was by my side, navigating the maze of medical appointments and treatments. This battle has been raging for over three years, and throughout it all, he's kept his struggle silent, his pain hidden.

I've never been one to hold back my feelings. My tears and fears were often laid bare in front of my medical team and friends. But what about him? Our home was a fortress of unspoken worries, a place where tears were strangers, kept at bay for the sake of our daughter and my parents. It wasn't until our friends, Dr Pragnesh and Dr Bijal, visited that I truly saw the toll it was taking on him. That day, Nitin broke down, revealing a glimpse of the immense pressure and pain he'd been carrying. It was a moment that peeled back the layers of his quiet resilience, exposing the depth of his love and his fears.

We made a pact, early on, to shield our daughter from the harsh realities of my condition. She was too young, we reasoned, to understand the gravity of it all. But the relentless progression of my illness brought a new urgency to share the truth with her. The thought of leaving her with misconceptions about my illness, should the worst happen, was unbearable. I wanted her to hear it from me, to know the full story without shadows or doubt.

So, on a sunny Sunday, I took her to the Swaminarayan temple by Tithal Beach, a place she loved for its sandy shores. After some time spent playing, we settled in the temple's canteen, Premvati, for a heart-to-heart. Even now, thinking back on that conversation gives me goosebumps. Nitin was hesitant; I could see it in his eyes. Yet, I was adamant. It was a conversation that needed to happen.

There, amidst the tranquillity of the temple and the gentle sounds of the beach, I shared my story with her. The pain of that moment was indescribable, but so was the strength it took to face it. Tears flowed freely, a river of shared sorrow and love. I tried to prepare her for a world that might one day not have me in it, to instil in her the strength to be independent, to be a support for her dad if ever he needed it.

It was undoubtedly one of the hardest things I've ever had to do. Yet, in that moment of vulnerability, we found a new kind of strength. A strength not just to face the challenges ahead, but to face them together, as a family united in love and resilience. This conversation, as painful as it was, underscored the importance of honesty, of preparing those we love for all possibilities, and of the incredible strength that lies within the bonds of family.

Chapter 5

The Visa Challenge

Our fight against the tumour hit a wall when we tried to get a US visa. Our first try didn't go well; we received a NO. Maybe it was because of our last name, Patel. People joked that Gujaratis like us would find any reason to go to the US and then never come back. So, when our visa application was rejected, Nitin and I felt our hopes crashing down. Our agent had told us, If they decide to give you the visa, they'll keep your passport. But that didn't happen. We walked out, forgetting our passport with the visa officer, feeling very down.

Right there, outside the US visa office, tears came. It hit us hard. With my aggressive tumour, we weren't just worried about the now but about what was coming. How long did I have? We didn't have any answers, and that scared us more than anything. It was a really tough time for both of us and our family, waiting to see what would happen next.

While waiting for our passports to return, we didn't just sit around. We made call after call, trying to figure out what to do. That's when we reached out to Dr Banavali, a senior consultant at Tata Hospital and the Head of the Paediatric unit. He conducted extensive research in chemotherapy, which has been globally recognised. He was the pioneer in India to propose non-surgical medical interventions to me. It was like a bit of luck finally came our way. We got an appointment for the same day we called.

After seeing him, we felt a bit of hope again. He added some new medicines to my treatment and planned for us to come back every six months. Even though my tumour kept growing, seeing my doctor gave us something to hold onto.

Dr. Banavali made every effort to treat my tumour, but unfortunately, it did not respond as expected. It continued to grow persistently, prompting us to consider reapplying for a US visa.

The first time, we were aiming for MD Anderson Hospital, known for being as good as Tata Hospital but in the US. The cost was huge, almost all our savings, but we thought if it could give me a chance at getting better, it might be worth it. If my current options don't work out, signing up with a hospital could let me join a drug trial. I know being a foreigner it's not easy but I wanted to try in case. Research in the US provides numerous approaches to address treatments. I delved into research and explored alternative treatments in the US from the Desmodian Facebook group. This new info got me thinking about reapplying for the visa, getting a second opinion, and trying out different ways to deal with this challenge.

Three months had passed since our first visa attempt fell flat. We were ready to try again, clinging to a sliver of hope that this time things might be different. That's when Malini Desai and her husband Raj stepped in, like unexpected heroes in our story. Malini was a childhood friend from school, someone I hadn't seen since our 12th standard. Life had taken us on different paths, and we hadn't spoken in years. Then, out of the blue, she came back into my life, needing treatment from me. It was during her visits that she learned about our struggle to get a US visa.

Malini's reappearance felt like fate. It was as if the universe was aligning to bring us the help we so desperately needed. Her husband Raj, who had experience with the visa process, offered to guide us. He sat down with us, showing us exactly how to correctly fill out the visa form this time. His guidance was like a light piercing through the fog, leading us through the intricate application process.

And then, the moment we'd been dreaming of finally came true. We got the visa. It wasn't just a win for us on our second try; it was a testament to the unbelievable kindness and support we received from friends like Malini and Raj. Their eagerness to be there for us, to offer a hand during this pivotal moment, was something we hadn't seen coming. It was a gift that meant more to us than words could express.

With the visa now in our hands, we started planning our journey to the USA, with one destination in mind: the Memorial Sloan Kettering International Cancer Center in New York. I came to know about the research works going on in this centre for desmoid tumours through my Desmodian group on Facebook. And they offered me a fee of only 300,000 rupees. Considering all these factors, we decided to visit this centre instead of the previous one. This place wasn't just a hospital; it was a ray of sunshine for people like me. We had heard its name spoken in awe in hospital corridors and seen it praised in online forums. It was famous for being at the forefront of cancer research and offering treatments that were not available anywhere else. This hospital represented a chance for us to take a different path in battling my stubborn tumour.

The thought of going there filled us with a mix of excitement and nervousness. What if this was the place where we would find the answer we had been searching for? The possibility made our hearts race. We were about to step into a world renowned for its medical breakthroughs, armed with nothing but our hope and the support of our incredible friends. It made us wonder what miracles might await us in New York. This question, this flicker of curiosity, is what kept us moving forward, eager to uncover the secrets that Memorial Sloan Kettering might hold for us.

Chapter 6

A New Hope in New York

Our arrival in New York marked the beginning of a chapter filled with anticipation and a glimmer of hope. The city, buzzing with life and energy, seemed to whisper promises of new possibilities. At the heart of our journey was the Memorial Sloan Kettering Cancer Center (MSK), a place where miracles are pursued daily. Here, I was about to meet someone who would change the course of my battle against the tumour.

Dr. M, an Indian sarcoma consultant at MSK, was renowned for his research on Desmoid Tumours. Learning that my consultant was not just an expert in his field but also shared my heritage brought an unexpected comfort. It felt like a sign, a nudge from the universe, that we had made the right decision.

Meeting Dr. M was like stumbling upon a guiding star in a long dark night. His presence was immediately comforting, and his genuine interest in my case was evident from the moment we began to speak. He listened to every word of my journey with such unwavering attention that it felt as if he was gathering each piece of my story, not just as a doctor, but as someone who truly cared. This level of empathy and understanding was something so profound, that it could have been the very inspiration I needed to pen down my journey.

As he absorbed my experiences, my struggles, and my fears, I felt seen and acknowledged in a way that was deeply moving. Our conversation, which spanned nearly an hour and a half, seemed to pause time itself. We dived deep into the intricacies of my condition, exploring every angle and possibility with meticulous care.

Dr. M laid out four potential treatment plans for me, a step-by-step approach to battle my illness. He suggested trying T. Sorafenib, a medication not yet available in India, as part of these strategies. The hitch was, they couldn't prescribe medication directly to someone from another country, which left us in a bit of a bind. However, just having these plans, knowing there were steps we could take if the current treatments failed, offered a ray of hope. It was comforting to know there was someone ready to help if we hit a dead end with the treatments back home.

Our week in New York was a strange mix of medical consultations and moments of unexpected joy. Our daughter, Naisargi, stayed back in India with my parents and in-laws, and the distance made our hearts grow fonder. We missed her terribly, so to bring back a piece of our journey, we picked out many gifts for her, imagining her delight as she opened each one.

In the evenings, Nitin and I found solace in the vibrant atmosphere of Times Square, just a stone's throw from our hotel. It became our little ritual, sitting there amidst the bustling crowd, soaking in the city's energy. The openness and liveliness of the people around us were infectious. We found ourselves getting lost in street performances—from dance to mono-acting, instrumental music, and mimicry. Each performance, each moment of laughter, was a precious distraction from the worries that weighed heavily on our minds.

The Warmth of Unexpected Friendships

Travelling to the USA, Nitin and I ventured into unknown territory, laden with anxiety and countless questions about what awaited us. It was a journey of firsts: our first time in the USA and our first time seeking treatment so far from home. The weight of our situation was heavy, filled with the kind of worries that keep you up at night.

In these times of uncertainty, my sister Vibhuti and her husband, both software engineers based in Pune at the time and now living in the USA, became our unsung heroes. Vibhuti dove into online research with a fervour, uncovering a Facebook support group named Desmodian. This group connected us with others facing similar battles across the globe, providing a platform to share experiences and find answers. It was Vibhuti's dedication that led us to one of the specialists at MSK, New York.

But the logistical challenges of staying in New York, especially under our unique circumstances, were daunting. Here, Dharini, a friend from another part of the USA, stepped in like a guardian. She not only booked a hotel for us in New York, considering my dietary restrictions and health needs but also ensured we had a microwave in our room—a small detail that meant the world to me.

Despite these arrangements, the shadows of worry lingered. What if the treatment didn't go as planned? Who would be there for Nitin if I needed more help than he could provide? It was in these moments of doubt that Heenaben Parekh emerged as a strong source of support. Working in my hospital back home, Heenaben was not just a colleague but a pillar within our community, known for her compassion and resourcefulness.

Understanding our predicament, Heenaben reached out to her network in the USA. It was then that Divya Jay Soni, a friend and distant relative of Heenaben, along with her husband Jay, extended an invitation that would deeply touch our hearts.

"Don't worry, we will take care of them," Divya assured. True to their word, Jay picked us up from our hotel and brought us to their home in New Jersey.

Divya and Jay were like angels to us. To them, we were not strangers but guests to be cherished and cared for. Divya prepared fresh Indian meals, considering my illness and dietary needs, with kindness and attention that brought tears to my eyes. Their hospitality didn't end with meals; they opened their home to us, providing comfort and a sense of family when we felt most alone. For three days, we were enveloped in their warmth and generosity, a brief respite before facing the challenges that lay ahead.

Even now, as I pen these words, the memory gives me goosebumps and brings tears to my eyes. 'Divya's generosity extended even further when she accompanied me to a store, where she helped me select toys and clothes for my daughter—a gesture so heartwarming and rare. Who would extend such kindness to strangers? Yet, this is the essence of our Gujarati spirit—ever ready to lend a hand. Thus, we returned to India, hearts brimming with hope, forever touched by the extraordinary kindness shown by those who were once strangers but became family.

Chapter 7

A Blend of Healing

Returning from the USA, I resumed my regular treatment under the watchful eye of Dr Banavali at Tata Hospital. Every six months, we would brace ourselves for the MRI results, hoping for a sign of improvement. My regimen consisted of T. Imatinib and T. Tamoxifen, a combination that, despite our hopes, wasn't making the difference we needed. The tumour remained stubbornly unresponsive. When Sorafenib, a newer molecule, became available in India, Dr Banavali decided it was time for a switch. Imatinib had run its course, and Sorafenib promised a new avenue of attack.

The transition to Sorafenib in 2018 marked the beginning of yet another chapter in this relentless struggle. Starting with a 200 mg dose, we gradually increased to 800 mg over 18 months, but the story was painfully familiar—my tumour remained indifferent to our efforts. With the introduction of Sorafenib, Tamoxifen along with Imatinib was phased out, deemed unwise for long-term use. However, Sorafenib brought its own battalion of side effects, each more challenging than the last.

Hair loss, high blood pressure, and the peeling of skin from my hands and feet turned daily life into a series of obstacles. My skin became so sensitive that walking became a trial, and my palms and soles burned with such intensity that only ice-cold water offered a brief respite. The hair loss was a blow I hadn't fully prepared for. Everyone said it was a benign disease, and that I wasn't undergoing traditional chemotherapy. Yet, there I was, holding clumps of hair after a bath, a silent testament to the battle raging within me.

Managing high blood pressure was another front in this war. I was on three different medications, taken three times a day, but my blood pressure readings were alarmingly high. My physician tirelessly adjusted doses and switched medications in an effort to bring it under control. Despite these Herculean efforts, the tumour continued its relentless expansion. Each MRI brought the same disheartening news: NO SIGN OF REGRESSION. We were fighting with everything we had, yet it felt like we were barely holding the line. You know, when you hear about cancer, there's often a plan or a story of someone who made it through. But with a rare disease, it's like walking into a thick fog without a clear path. There's no guide, no success stories to follow, just a lot of unanswered questions. It's like being on a journey with no end in sight, facing unexpected challenges without any warning. Even after doing everything possible, you're left wondering what's going to happen next. It's hard to accept that some things are just out of our hands.

This period of my treatment was a testament to persistence in the face of seemingly insurmountable challenges. My family and I were united in our efforts, each of us contributing to the battle in our own way. Yet, the tumour's resistance to treatment was a stark reminder of the unpredictability and cruelty of this disease. We were not just waiting for a breakthrough; we were waiting for a sunrise, a new day that would bring hope and a sign that our efforts were not in vain.

As the months rolled by with no sign of regression from the allopathic treatments, it became clear that we needed to cast our net wider. In 2018, spurred by a mix of desperation and hope, we turned our gaze towards alternative treatments, starting with Ayurveda. My sister Vaishali and her husband Ketan Patel introduced me to an Ayurvedic doctor in Surat, where I started a Panchakarma journey, followed by Shuddhikaran—purification of the body. The regimen was tough, involving strict diet plans that felt more like a test of will than treatment. I was to eat only a specific item for a week, then switch to liquids the next. Add to this the use of cow ghee in my nose and umbilicus, among other practices. I dove into these pieces of advice with blind faith, clinging to the hope of finding relief.

During this period, my father and a few friends brought up the possibility of Tibetan medicine. It was an unconventional path, met with scepticism but driven by the urgency of our situation, Nitin and I found ourselves on a journey to a Tibetan clinic. The process was alien to us; after a 48-hour wait for our appointment, the doctors merely glanced at my reports, conversing in Tibetan before prescribing medicines in a language we couldn't decipher. Despite the strangeness of it all, I committed to this new treatment, taking Tibetan drugs alongside my Ayurvedic and allopathic medications.

My daily routine became a rigorous schedule of pills—three Ayurvedic tablets four times a day, four Tibetan tablets four times a day, and my allopathic tablets. On top of this, I started consuming wheatgrass juice, homegrown by my mother. Amidst suggestions from well-meaning friends and a naturopathy doctor, she took it upon herself to cultivate seven pots of wheatgrass, one for each day of the week. The process wasn't easy, but her love and dedication infused each glass of juice with something more potent than the nutrients it held.

My in-laws contributed too, bringing various roots and herbs, each with the promise of health. It seemed everyone had something to offer, a testament to their love and concern. My family, ever-present, became a constant rotation of caregivers, offering medicine, juice, fruits, and more every half hour. But the burden of their well-intentioned efforts eventually became too much.

One day, overwhelmed by the constant attention and the sheer volume of remedies, I snapped, pleading for a break from the relentless medication regimen. By April 2019, amidst the maximum dose of Sorafenib, I was struck down by a high-grade fever. After days of oral treatments failed to make a dent, a 15-day hospital stay ensued. Despite the best efforts of my physician, the fever persisted, stubbornly resistant to treatment. All my reports came back normal, deepening the frustration. We sought help from a renowned cancer hospital – Tata Hospital in Mumbai, only to find there were no beds available. Told to return the next day, my frustration boiled over. Exhausted and disheartened, I chose to return home instead.

So, at that point, in a moment of despair, I actually asked my husband for a break, a pause from all the treatments and hospital visits, which seemed never-ending. This whole journey had really taken a toll on me, not just physically but emotionally and spiritually too. My family was okay with me taking a break from all the treatments and hospital visits, but we wanted to make sure it was alright with my doctor at Memorial Sloan Kettering Cancer Hospital in New York. So, we set up an online chat with him, and he gave us the green light. He did warn us, though, that because my disease was so tough, I'd probably need to start injectable chemotherapy at some point. I was ready for anything by then.

There was this one thing I really wanted to do—I asked Nitin to take me to Ambaji, a place in Gujarat known for its powerful temple, one of the Shaktipiths. There's this part of the temple, the Garbhgruh, that's usually off-limits unless you have special permission. My cousin, Gunvantbhai, managed to arrange that for us, so I could be right there, up close to MAA Amba.

Standing there in front of MAA, something in me just broke open. I cried like I hadn't cried before, pouring out all my fear, my pain, and my hopes right there. It was the first time I truly let go and surrendered—not just my illness but myself—to MAA Amba. I begged her for relief, asking her to either take me away from this suffering or to grant me a life free from this disease. I was at the end of my rope, asking for peace, either in this life or beyond.

That moment in the temple, crying out to MAA Amba was a turning point for me. It was when I stopped trying to control the outcome and just laid all my burdens down at her feet. It was a mix of desperation and faith, but somehow, it gave me a kind of peace I hadn't felt in a long time. It was as if, by surrendering, I'd lifted the weight off my shoulders and placed it into hands far more capable than my own. Following this pivotal experience, I decided to take a break from my ongoing medical treatment. Dr. Banavali recommended an MRI after three months to ensure close monitoring of my condition. To everyone's astonishment, the MRI revealed that my 4x4 cm tumour had completely disappeared. This unexpected turn of events felt nothing short of miraculous to me, my family, and everyone involved, highlighting the profound impact of faith and surrender.

Chapter 8

Spiritual Journey to Healing

The 18 months following my diagnosis were a blur of treatments, hospital visits, and relentless attempts to find something—anything—that might stem the tide of my aggressive tumour. High doses of medication became my daily routine, with my doctors exploring every possible avenue for my recovery, yet without certainty of what might work. In this uncertainty, I chose to follow their guidance without question, but a part of me yearned for more, for any additional thread of hope to cling to. Yet, the brief appearance of the miraculous ''nil report' was only a temporary relief in my ongoing struggle.

It was during this time of desperation that alternative paths to healing began to unfold before me. My in-laws introduced me to Reiki, a form of energy healing, and suggested consulting an astrologer for additional insights. Sceptical but open-minded, I decided to explore these avenues. After all, in the face of such a relentless adversary, what harm was there in seeking out every potential ally?

My sister Vaishali brought to my attention the concept of energy exchange, suggesting that my ailment might be the result of an imbalance or dominance of negative energy within me. She led me to someone who specialised in this form of healing, promising an exchange of energy that could potentially shift the tide in my favour. It might sound far-fetched to some, but when you're grappling with a life-altering diagnosis, you find yourself willing to try anything.

And so, I found myself delving into practices that I never would have considered before. I was instructed to write positive affirmations 100 times, five per day, a task I undertook with diligence. It was a practice rooted in the belief that you can transform your reality with your thoughts, and that sending positive signals to your cells could indeed foster regeneration and healing. This idea, once foreign to me, began to resonate deeply. The act of writing those affirmations became a daily ritual, one that offered a sense of control and contribution to my own healing process.

My journey took an interesting turn when my sister, Vaishali, with my sister-in-law Anitaben and brother-in-law Kamleshbhai, suggested that I should see an astrologer we knew from years ago. I met him when I was 30, at a time when I was trying hard to have a baby and not succeeding. He had warned me about possible gut problems in the future. Back then, I laughed it off. I thought my stomach was strong enough to handle any kind of street food.

Years later, that same astrologer recommended I wear a Tiger Claw set in gold for protection. But finding a real Tiger Claw is tough in India because they're banned. That's when Chirag Shah, someone I worked with, came into the picture. He had one, and I was curious about where he got it. It turned out his brother had sent it to him from abroad.

Chirag didn't just tell me this; he went a step further. He got in touch with his brother and arranged for a Tiger Claw to be sent to me, insisting it be a gift. He said it had to be given from the heart to work its magic. I was touched by his kindness. Despite being much younger, Chirag showed a generosity that was deeply moving. He and his brother, who were almost strangers to me, played a significant role in my path to getting better.

Wearing the eleven Mukhi Rudraksha, putting on the Kumkum Tikka, and the Crystal Mala around my neck every day became a part of my routine. Each item was chosen for its healing properties. Even though I often wondered about the science behind these practices, the part of me desperate to get better clung to them. It was the kindness and positive energy from people like Chirag that really made a difference in my recovery.

I've kept up with these rituals, not because I'm convinced they work miracles on my body, but because they've woven themselves into the fabric of my spiritual quest. These practices have opened my eyes to the immense power of belief, the unyielding force of hope, and the critical role a positive outlook plays when life throws challenges your way. This journey for me hasn't just been about seeking ways to heal physically but has evolved into a deeper quest for inner peace and resilience.

Initially, I doubted the benefits of these practices. The logic in me questioned their effectiveness, pondering, How is this going to help? Yet, there was no downside to trying them; they weren't going to harm me. So, I thought, Why not? Encouraged by the suggestions of those close to me, I decided to give almost everything a shot. This openness to experiment has been a cornerstone of my journey, teaching me more about myself and the world around me than I could have imagined.

Healing involves addressing the root cause of a disease. It is believed that many illnesses are psychosomatic, stemming from long-held mental trauma or grudges that manifest as physical ailments. The journey towards healing has been full of surprises, blending the worlds of science and spirituality in ways I hadn't anticipated. It's been a powerful reminder that healing doesn't just come from medical treatments; it's also about the energy we're surrounded by and the beliefs we carry in our hearts.

Throughout this journey, I 'didn't put my life on pause. I continued my work as an obstetrician, and the support I received from my staff was incredible. They did so much more than their job descriptions; they carried hope for me in their hearts. My Christian staff members visited Mother 'Mary's church to pray for me, while my Hindu colleagues undertook Parnera hikes and visited temples, always keeping me in their prayers for a speedy recovery. I felt incredibly blessed by their acts of faith.

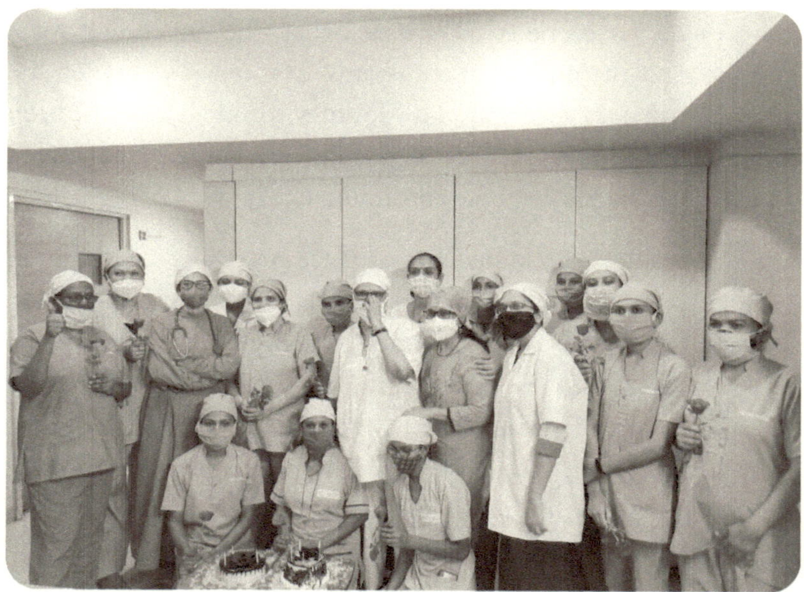

Even during my time in the OPD, patients would notice the changes in my appearance, like the thinning of my hair, and express their concerns. They'd ask if I was okay, wondering if I had typhoid or cancer. I'd respond vaguely, acknowledging their concern without delving into details. Among these caring souls was a patient of mine who, after 15 years of infertility, had twins thanks to IVF treatment under my care. She took her gratitude a step further by making a vow to her family deity, Kuldevi, for my health. Remembering my follow-up dates better than I did, she would check in on me before and after each appointment. When my reports finally showed no signs of disease, she took a flight—despite the financial burden and the need to leave her 3-year-old twins with a neighbour—to offer prayers and thanks at her Kuldevi's temple on my behalf. Mrs Venilla's dedication and the lengths she went to for me are something I will always be deeply thankful for.

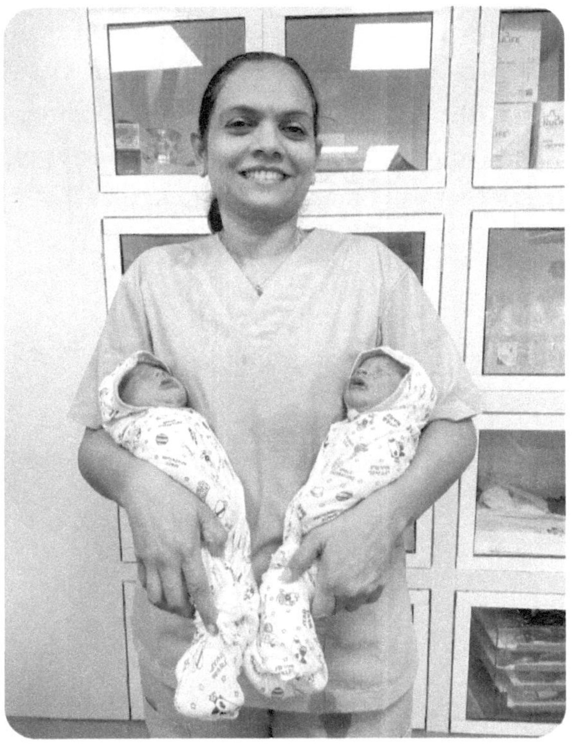

My cousins Jayshreeben and Leenaben arranged a meeting with Mahant Swami of the Swaminarayan community. The Swaminarayan community typically does not meet with females, as they are not allowed near the saints. Despite being a woman of practical empowerment, I initially hesitated. However, I set aside my reservations and permitted Nitin to go in my place. He engaged in a 15-minute personal conversation on my behalf. I felt fortunate to indirectly receive his blessings. Mahant Swami requested Nitin to visit the Swaminarayan temple every full moon for 11 months. Consequently, Nitin and I went on a 100-kilometre journey every full moon for darshan.

This road to recovery has taught me that healing is a multifaceted journey. It's not just the medical treatments that count but also the compassion, prayers, and positive energy from the people around us. Their faith, combined with my professional knowledge, has shown me that the true essence of healing encompasses much more than just the physical aspect—it's a blend of support, love, and spirituality that truly makes a difference.

Chapter 9

A Community of Healing

The day I broke down, the late Dr. Purnima Nadkarni, whose wisdom and kindness I miss, saw my distress. She gently guided me to the Brahma Kumaris' Centre in Pardi. It was there, amidst the serene surroundings, that I started a life-changing seven-day course on Rajyoga meditation. This wasn't just about learning to meditate; it was an education in life itself. The course illuminated the concepts of our life cycle, the intricate dance of karma, and the art of acceptance—embracing things as they are when change is beyond reach and taking action when it's within our grasp.

One of the most profound lessons was about creating a 'No anger zone'—a sanctuary within myself where calm and peace could flourish, unaffected by the external chaos. The teachings went deeper, showing me how to connect with God, maintain a state of calm, and cultivate happiness regardless of circumstances. Inspired by this newfound knowledge, I began seeking out Brahma Kumaris' programmes wherever I could, drawn to the wisdom of BK Shivani. Her words, her energy, it all resonated with me on a level I couldn't quite explain.

I had the chance to attend a conference at the BK centre in Manesar, near Delhi. Contrary to what one might expect from the bustling capital, this place was a haven of peace. The sight of peacocks dancing and the sound of birds chirping in the morning were ethereal, almost surreal. It was an environment that echoed with positive energy, a testament to the transformative power of the place.

No matter where BK Shivanididi was speaking, I made it a point to be there. Each lecture and each seminar was an opportunity to learn something new, to feel connected not just to her but to a larger, invisible energy that bound us all. This connection wasn't just in my head; it was palpable, a real force that I, sitting in the audience, could feel emanating from her on stage. This compelling energy is what keeps drawing me back to her sessions and to the BK centre in Killa Pardi.

Regular visits became a part of my routine, each one reinforcing the lessons of peace, calm, and happiness. It's a bit hard to put into words, and I know it might not resonate with everyone. But for me, these experiences have been life-changing. They've shown me that even amidst the greatest storms, there can be a centre of peace within, a sanctuary where I can retreat and find strength. This journey with the Brahma Kumaris has been about more than just finding peace; it's been about rediscovering life, and learning to live it with a serenity I never knew was possible.

Yoga and meditation became my new best friends. It was my folks who nudged me towards it, thinking it'd help my body. But it did so much more for my mind. A temple priest recommended the Mrityunjay Jaap, and my Bhabhi brought in the Ram Ram Jaap. Starting my day with these chants, I began to see a change in myself. I was spending time with myself, really listening to what I needed, which, to be honest, felt a bit selfish at first. But then it hit me—looking after yourself isn't selfish. It's necessary.

This whole journey taught me about the power of our subconscious mind—a concept I hadn't given much thought to before. My yoga teacher explained how physical exercise primes you for deeper meditation, making it easier to quiet down the whirlwind of thoughts and focus on the present. She was right. Hitting the mat early in the morning, when the world's still quiet, I found a space where I could truly connect with myself.

What I've realised is that community—whether it's the BKs, my family pushing me towards yoga, or the virtual support from my brother-in-law—plays a huge role in healing. It's not just about the physical stuff, like getting rid of symptoms. It's the feeling of not being alone, of having people who get what you're going through, and who stand with you, cheering you on, and sometimes, giving you that nudge you need to keep moving forward. This chapter of my life has been about discovering that healing is a team sport, and I'm so grateful for my team.

Chapter 10

The Power of Mantras

Growing up, I never paid much attention to all the spiritual stuff that was part of our Indian culture. We always think the West has it all figured out, that our ways are old and not that cool. But when life got tough, I realised how wrong I was. Our traditions are like hidden gems, full of wisdom on how to live a good life. It's funny how we only turn to them when we hit a rough patch, instead of making them a part of our everyday life.

I recall coming across advice that when life presents challenges, it's best to confront them directly without hesitation. It's like being stuck in a river. You can't just stand there; you have to swim to reach the shore. It clicked with me that waiting around for someone else to save me wasn't an option. I had to find my own way out of the mess.

That's when I really got into chanting mantras. The Mrityunjaya Jaap was the first one I tried. The Mahamrityunjaya Mantra is a verse from the Rig Veda and is considered to be the most powerful Shiva Mantra. It bestows longevity and wards off calamities. It also removes fears and heals holistically. This eternal mantra is also a part of the Yajurveda.

So, I started chanting it every day. A priest told me if I could do it 350,000 times, it would make a big difference. It took me 18 months, but I did it. We even had a big ceremony at the end, which felt pretty special with my staff and family.

Then there was the Hanuman Chalisa and the Durga Chalisa. The Hanuman Chalisa is supposed to kick out all the negativity and give you strength. The Durga Chalisa is more about keeping you well. My mom still chants it for me every day. Through the power of mantras, you connect with the divine essence – GOD. These mantras help you tune into your self-awareness, connecting you with your subconscious. It's like diving into your inner self, uncovering deep insights about your body, spotting areas for growth and things that need fixing.

Getting into these mantras changed a lot for me. They were like a steady hand on my back, pushing me through the tough times. I learned that these old practices from our culture are not just about faith; they're about finding strength within yourself, about facing life with a bit of extra armour.

When I first started chanting mantras, it was more out of curiosity than anything else—someone suggested it, and I thought, Why not? It was like being a kid again, listening and following along without much questioning, simply because it felt like there was nothing to lose. But as time went on, something started to shift inside me. My anxiety, which had been like a constant, unwelcome companion, began to ease up. Despite my tumour growing, I found myself feeling more at peace, more settled than I had in a long time.

I used to have this rapid pulse all the time, something my doctor said was due to anxiety, and I was on medication just to manage that. But as I kept up with my daily mantras, I noticed my pulse calming down, and my blood pressure started to stabilise too. It was as if acknowledging the problem and facing it with these mantras was helping my body find its balance again.

This newfound calm wasn't just about feeling less anxious; it made me more confident and more resilient. It was as if some kind of divine energy was working through me, easing my worries and making me stronger. Before I knew it, these practices had woven themselves into the fabric of my life, becoming something I couldn't imagine going without. Even now, if I skip my morning routine, I feel off, like I've missed an important step in starting my day.

My terrace garden has always been my sanctuary, a slice of nature right at home. Being there, amidst the spinach, fenugreek, brinjal, tomatoes, cauliflower, and many other vegetables I've grown myself, fills me with an indescribable joy. There's something profoundly powerful about watching these plants grow, about being surrounded by the greenery. It's a reminder of nature's strength and its capacity to bring happiness into our lives. Every day, without fail, I make time to connect with this little piece of nature. It's not just about the fresh, oxygen-rich air or the cool breeze; it's about the happiness and tranquillity that envelops me when I'm there.

This connection to nature reminds me of how I began practising Pranayama and yoga. My friends and I supported each other in many ways. Pranayama was one of those supports, teaching us the importance of breathing fully. My friend and I learned that our everyday shallow breaths fail to open the distant alveoli in our lungs, leading to less oxygen absorption and the accumulation of free radicals, which could cause diseases. Regular practice of Pranayama could enhance oxygen intake, aiding in cell regeneration and overall well-being.

This journey with mantras and morning rituals taught me the true power of routine in healing. It's not just about the physical actions but the mental and spiritual rejuvenation that comes from consistent practice. It's a reminder that sometimes, the simplest acts—like chanting a mantra or sitting in the sun—can have the most profound impact on our well-being. It showed me that healing is as much about nurturing the soul as it is about treating the body.

Chapter 11

Reconnecting with Earth

Lately, I've started walking barefoot, letting my feet touch the ground, really feeling the earth beneath me. They call this grounding or earthing, and it's all about reconnecting with the earth's natural energy. Sounds a bit out there, right? But there's actual science behind it, saying that the earth's electrical charge can help out our bodies in a bunch of ways.

Then there's just being out in nature. It's like nature has this quiet way of making you feel better, just by being around it. I took that to heart and began spending as much time outside as I could. It's like the more I was out there, the more I felt like myself again.

My dad once told me about a doctor from his younger days who had blood cancer. Back then, treatments weren't what they are today, so the guy turned to Tibetan medicine. He used to travel by train all the way to Mcleodganj to get his meds, which meant he was on the road a lot, turning each trip into a month-long journey. But get this—the guy lived to be 90. My dad used this story to nudge me towards spending time in the Himalayas instead of typical holiday spots. And honestly, it made sense.

Following my dad's advice turned out to be a game-changer for me. He always said there's something special about the Himalayas, some kind of energy that just makes you feel better, more alive. And he was right. Since 2018, I've made it a point to visit the

Himalayas twice a year, and since my daughter started studying there in 2021, I found myself drawn there every couple of months.

Back in 2019, right before the world turned upside down with the pandemic, I took a leap and went on my first big trip to the Do Dham. Some folks said, "Wait until you're older", or "You need to be fit for this kind of adventure." But hey, life's too short, right? So off I went to Yamunotri and Gangotri, and honestly, words fall short trying to describe those places. And then there's Haridwar, with its Har Ki Pauri—it's just something else. Sitting by the Ganga, Nitin and I could spend forever just soaking it all in. We caught the Ganga Aarti more times than I can count, and each time, it hit us—a kind of powerful vibe that's tough to put into words.

This trip was so much more than just checking places off a bucket list. It felt like stepping into a world where every corner, every turn, has a story, a vibe of its own. The Himalayas? They're not just mountains. They're this age-old place of peace where people have been finding themselves, you know? They talk about these mountains like they're alive, whispering secrets about life and what's beyond. Uttarakhand, with its nickname 'Devbhoomi,' really lives up to the hype, making you feel like you've stepped into a whole different world.

When the lockdown hit, I already had plans in my mind for visiting Kedarnath and Badrinath. The moment travel restrictions eased a bit, I didn't hesitate. I booked my tickets and went. Thankfully, I had a smooth and safe darshan, even amidst the pandemic. And as soon as the second wave's lockdown lifted in June, I was off to Kashmir. My heart always leans towards the Himalayas whenever I'm planning a trip. There were times I wasn't feeling my best, questioning whether I should travel. But each time, I returned feeling recharged, healthier, and more convinced than ever in the healing power of nature.

Throughout this journey, books have become my sanctuary, each one offering its own kind of medicine. It all started with "You Can Heal Your Life" by Louise Hay. This book opened my eyes to the idea that our thoughts and words have the power to shape our reality. From there, I dived into "The Power of Subconscious Mind" by Joseph Murphy, which taught me how our deeper mind influences our life and health. "Life's Amazing Secrets" by Gaur Gopaldas gave me a fresh perspective on balancing life's different aspects, while "The Secret" by Rhonda Byrne introduced me to the law of attraction, reinforcing the belief that we attract what we focus on.

"Autobiography of a Yogi" took me on a spiritual adventure, showing me the depth of Indian spirituality and its masters. "Healed" by Manisha Koirala was a personal account of battling cancer, which I found incredibly moving and relatable. Along with these, I found solace and inspiration in many Gujarati books, each adding to my reservoir of hope and positivity.

These books collectively taught me the importance of nurturing positive thoughts, visualising the life I wanted, and understanding the immense influence our subconscious mind holds over our well-being. I learned that holding onto grudges or unresolved trauma can manifest as a physical disease by sending negative signals to our cells. To counter this, I started filling my mind with positive thoughts and vibrations, consciously releasing any held grudges and learning to embrace happiness in its purest form.

The celebration became a key part of our lives, never missing a chance to find joy in even the smallest moments at home. This attitude of constant positivity wasn't just for me; it enveloped everyone around me, from family and friends to those who were tirelessly working to improve my health.

One of the highlights during this period was a trip to Europe in 2019 for an infertility conference, a dream I had long harboured but seemed impossible given my health. My friend Dr. Ranjeeta, understanding how much it meant to me, promised my family she would take care of me. It was an unforgettable experience, not just for the knowledge gained but for the sheer joy of being able to fulfil a dream against the odds. I even carried injections with me, just in case, but the trip itself was a testament to the fact that with a bit of courage and a lot of support, anything is possible.

This journey with books and the occasional escape into new experiences taught me a fundamental truth: healing is as much about the mind as it is about the body. By feeding my mind with inspiring stories, practical wisdom, and transformative ideas, I was able to cultivate a garden of positivity that sustained me through the toughest times, reinforcing my belief in the power of hope, the strength of faith, and the endless possibilities that life offers, even in the face of adversity.

Chapter 12

Embracing Life

During this whole rollercoaster with my illness, I found myself turning to gardening, letting my hands get dirty, and really connecting with the earth. It's funny how planting a seed, watering it, and watching it grow can make you feel so alive. It's like each plant was a little reminder that life keeps pushing through, no matter what.

Balancing my work life through all of this wasn't easy, but I never stopped working. A big part of that was thanks to my patients, the late Dr. Purnima Nadkarni, and the amazing staff at my hospital. They all had my back, supporting me in more ways than I could count.

My patients were my rock. Their support, their prayers, and even their fasting on my behalf gave me the strength to keep fighting. Some went to holy places for me, hoping for my recovery. There was even one patient who, when she heard my reports came back normal, flew to her native place just to give thanks. She didn't have much, but she did that for me. Every time I think about it, I get goosebumps.

Writing about this journey, and reliving the toughest parts of my life, is no easy task. But I'm doing it for folks out there who are clinging to life, searching for hope.

My message is simple:

Never give up.

Be as stubborn as the weeds in your garden,

Keep trying, no matter what.

Fight with everything you've got until the very end. Who knows? Maybe that determination, that refusal to surrender, will be what turns the tide.

It's about not just accepting what's handed to you but interacting with the world, engaging with life even when it feels like you're running on empty. My patients, their concern, and their actions on my behalf, they taught me the true meaning of support and community. And in doing so, they showed me that surrendering to a higher power, rather than to my illness, was the path I needed to take. It's a journey of patient acceptance, of learning to live fully in the moment, and of never, ever giving up hope.

Chapter 13

The Unbreakable Bond

I'm standing strong today, and if you ask me why, the answer's simple—my family. They've been my fortress, my constant in a sea of uncertainty.

In silence, his love speaks a universe, fasting for me, his quiet strength my verse.

My husband, with his quiet strength, has been my rock. He's not one for grand gestures or too many words, but his actions speak volumes. Managing our lives, from taking care of me and our daughter to keeping our finances afloat, he's done it all with a grace that leaves me in awe. And every Saturday, for the past seven years, he fasts for me, a practice suggested by an astrologer. It's these acts of faith, of love, that make me feel truly blessed.

In every whispered prayer and silent stride, my parents' love, a boundless tide.

Then there's my dad, my steadfast guardian, who's been beside us through every surgery and complication, offering not just emotional but unwavering practical support. My mom, though not the one to talk much, has poured her heart into prayers for me, chanting mantras, Mrityunjay Jaap, Durga Chalisa, and more, believing in the power of each word for my healing.

In storms, one stands by my bed, another navigates the sea, and the youngest shows wisdom's thread—sisters, my lighthouse trio, guiding me.

My sister Vaishali and her husband Ketan were a constant presence, standing by me through every hospital stay, never letting her duties as a mother to her own daughter hinder her support for me. Vibhuti and Dipak, with their knack for navigating the digital world, took charge of coordinating my consultations in the USA, handling everything from scheduling to payments. Megha and

Bipin, the youngest ones, displayed remarkable maturity, playing pivotal roles in guiding our family through this challenging storm. My cousin Falguni and her brother Jignesh selflessly looked after our children Naisargi, Zia, Kiana, and Varnica without needing to be asked, for which we are truly grateful.

April 2019 was perhaps the darkest hour, with doctors giving up hope. At that time, my parents and daughter were in the USA, leaving my sisters and their husbands to juggle their jobs from Vapi to Surat, ensuring one pair was always with me, day or night. Their presence, their willingness to do anything and everything to ease my pain, was a testament to the depth of our bond.

In shadows deep, they crossed the miles, with silent strength and hopeful smiles. Through every trial, their spirits kindle, guiding lights that softly twinkle. Together, we face the darkest nights, their friendship, my unwavering light.

Dipak travelled all the way to Ahmedabad for my surgery, embodying the true spirit of family. Pinki, Nimesh, and Himanshu Rana stood by me during my major surgery in Ahmedabad, with Hasu opening her home to me during my follow-ups. I'm forever grateful for Gitesh and his mom, who, despite her own battle with cancer, was a wellspring of motivation.

When I was on what everyone thought was my deathbed, my family across the globe united in prayer, chanting the Mrityunjay in unison, weaving a protective web of hope around me.

In your smile, my world finds its glow,
A heart of gold, in you, does show.
Through every high and every low,
My love for you will forever grow.

Naisargi, our daughter, has been amazing through all of this. Whenever me and Nitin had to go for my treatments, she stayed with her grandparents without any fuss. She never complained or felt sad when we had to leave her. Then, in April 2019, while she was in the US for summer vacation with her aunt, and I was back home struggling with a fever that just wouldn't break, everyone started chanting Mrityunjay Jaap for me. Naisargi, seeing this, joined in on her own, without anyone asking her to. It was a big moment, showing how brave and caring she is, just like the rest of our family.

This whole experience brought our family even closer, making us a solid team. The kindness and sacrifices from everyone really showed how much we stick together through thick and thin. My family has been my rock, always there for me during the tough times. Their support gave me the push I needed to keep going. With them by my side, I felt ready to take on anything, knowing we're stronger when we're together.

Chapter 14

Looking Back

Now, five years into being disease-free, when I look back at my journey, a deep sense of pride wells up inside me. Over the years, I've faced countless moments where I was told I might not make it. Right after my surgery, I hit a major setback with intestinal obstruction and lost a significant amount of weight, putting my survival into question. Again in 2019, battling a fever that no one could diagnose, whispers circulated that I was on my deathbed. But not once did I entertain the thought of giving up.

This relentless will to live, to push through the pain and fear, I see now, was my inner strength at play. It's a realisation that has only deepened over time. My desire to survive, to overcome every hurdle thrown my way, is the reason I'm still here, sharing my story.

The journey wasn't just marked by illness but also by the countless scans and procedures—six CT scans, one PET scan, and thirteen MRI scans, to be precise. Each session on the MRI table, which could last up to two hours, was a trial in itself. The process, involving oral, IV, and sometimes rectal contrasts, was far from easy. Being in that room, trying to follow the technician's instructions to breathe in, breathe out, and hold my breath, all while feeling the warm rush of contrast fluid through my veins, was overwhelming. The coldness of the room, coupled with the anxiety of the moment, made each session an ordeal only those who've gone through it can truly understand.

Writing this book wasn't just a way to share my own hard times. It was also about shining a light on the stories of my fellow Desmodians, a group of us battling the same rare condition. Their struggles, filled with uncertainty, fear, and unbelievable pain, are stories that need to be told. And it's not just about the pain. It's about the incredible people who stand by us, giving their all to help us through each day.

There's this one young guy, only 16, who's been fighting a tumour in his knee since he was just nine. Imagine, after all the treatments and attempts to beat it, he's still confined to his bed. The thought of his parents, seeing their son stuck in bed day after day, is just heart-wrenching. Then, there's another person dealing with a tumour that has taken over his entire pelvis, turning the simple act of going to the bathroom into a major ordeal. And there's someone who went through two huge surgeries, losing 10 litres of blood, and surviving thanks to 25 blood transfusions.

These stories are only a glimpse of what Desmodians face. Each of us has our own journey of fighting against the odds. My story, filled with its own challenges and moments of despair, also speaks to the resilience of the human spirit, the strength of hope, and our unyielding desire to keep living. This narrative isn't just mine to tell. It's for every Desmodian or anyone walking this tough path, offering a bit of understanding, a sense of connection, and maybe, a little strength to keep fighting.

During my treatment, the doctors were upfront: "Don't expect a cure. If we can keep your disease stable, that's a victory." It wasn't until I connected with other Desmodians on social media that I realised how fortunate I was. When I asked my doctor about my own prognosis, his honesty was chilling: "It's usually considered benign, but there's a debate—some say it's a low-grade sarcoma. Surgery might be our only option, but how many times can we operate?"

This disease, it's a monster hiding in plain sight. Touch it, and it might just grow back angrier. When it's deep in the abdomen or pelvis, like mine, surgery becomes a gamble with diminishing returns. I've heard stories of others in our community undergoing multiple surgeries, only to end up battling malabsorption and intestinal blockages.

I count myself among the lucky ones. My ordeal seemed to end in 2019, a miraculous turn in my story. Being a doctor myself, I've experienced both sides of this disease—the professional and the personal. My stubbornness, refusing to let this tumour define my life, has shown me a resilience I never knew I had.

Our community is small, with a couple of hundred Desmodians across the country, all of us navigating this uncertain path. This disease is unpredictable; it doesn't necessarily shorten life but complicates it in ways difficult to imagine. My recurrence came just 11 months after surgery, a stark reminder of the ongoing battle we face.

So here I am, a few years down the line, and my life's taken turns I never saw coming. If you'd told me before all this that I'd find a kind of quiet strength from battling a disease, I might've laughed. But that's exactly what happened. This whole thing has been like digging deep into a well I didn't know I had, pulling up bucketfuls of grit and hope I never knew I owned.

Right now, my disease is kind of like a quiet roommate living around my aorta. It's been keeping to itself, not causing trouble for the last three years. And I'm thankful for that peace, but there's always that little voice wondering, What if it wakes up?

Life's got its routines, like those iron and Vitamin B12 shots I line up for every six months, or dealing with days when my stomach decides it's running the show. Then there's watching clumps of hair go down the drain and feeling my hands and feet burn as if I've walked through fire, thanks to all the nerve damage. Sounds tough, right? But when I hear what some folks are going through, my heart just goes out to them, and suddenly, my troubles don't seem so big.

What's really changed for me is figuring out how tough I can be. It's like I've got this inner muscle that's gotten really strong through all this. I look at problems now, and where I used to see walls, I see hurdles. High ones, sure, but not impossible to get over.

Looking to the future? I'm cautiously hopeful. I've got this mix of let's do this and what's next? going on. The disease is still a part of my life, but it's not the whole story. It's more like a chapter that's made me who I am today—someone who knows the value of a good day, who cherishes laughs a little louder, hugs a little tighter, and loves a little deeper.

Late Dr. Purnima Nadkarni was a beacon of strength on my journey, shining brightly even when things got tough. She bravely fought against a severe form of cancer discovered in 2021. Despite my best efforts to support her, we sadly lost her in 2021. Together, we put up a fierce fight for her, but it taught us the unpredictable nature of life.

Now, my routine includes an annual MRI, iron injections every six months, and monthly vitamin B12 shots. It's been five years since I've needed any medication, though I'm aware my condition, desmoid, could change at any moment. But I'm equipped with knowledge and ready to face whatever comes my way.

The road ahead is unknown, and yeah, that can be scary. But I'm walking into it with my head held high and a heart full of hope, carrying the strength and lessons I've picked up along the way. This journey has shown me life's fragile beauty and the incredible power of the human spirit. Amidst it all, I've learned to never give up, to fight, fight until I succeed. Being stubborn has become my armour, teaching me not to surrender to the disease but to surrender to God instead.

As Rainer Maria Rilke once said, "Let everything happen to you: beauty and terror." Just keep going. No feeling is final. With this in mind, I'm not just surviving; I'm living, really living, embracing both the mess and magic that life throws my way, knowing that no feeling is final and the journey is worth every step.

B. J. MEDICAL COLLEGE
AHMEDABAD
ESTD. 1949
STAR
MONTH
CONGRATULATIONS
STAR
MONTH
CONGRATULATIONS
ANAMIKA PATEL